MW00720325

Lots of Time Left

A Journal by Dr.Martin Verhoeven, Ph.D

LOTS OF TIME LEFT

A Journal by
Martin Verhoeven

Buddhist Text Translation Society
Dharma Realm Buddhist University
Dharma Realm Buddhist Association
Burlingame California
USA

Published by:

> Buddhist Text Translation Society
> 1777 Murchison Drive
> Burlingame, CA 94010-4504

© 2003   Buddhist Text Translation Society
> Dharma Realm Buddhist University
> Dharma Realm Buddhist Association

First Printing: 1977
Second Printing: 2003

Printed in Taiwan

Library of Congress Cataloging-in-Publication Data

Verhoeven, Martin.
Lots of time left / by Martin Verhoeven.
    p. cm.
Includes index.
ISBN 0-88139-488-2 (alk. paper)
1. Verhoeven, Martin. 2. Buddhists—United States—
Biography. 3. Hsèuan Hua, 1908- 4. Spiritual biography—
United States. 5. Spiritual life—Buddhism. I. Title.

BQ994.E74 A3 2002
294.3'92'092—dc21

                                    2002007275

Content

Marty's Journal 1

Decision To Go To Gold Mountain 8

Great Compassion Session 10

Decision to take Refuge 15

Dream Number One 20

Dream Number Two 24

Dream Number Three 29

After the Session 32

Ceremony for Taking the Dead Across 35

Dream of My Grandfather 37

Ghost in the House 39

Dreams and Magic Spells 41

Vows 44

Precepts ....."Right On Time." 47

Ch'an Session 55

Ch'an Session Brat 57

Bodhisattva Precepts 60

Amitabha Session 64

Earthquake Dream 69

Earthquake Vows 73

Filiality 76

Pt. Reyes Mantra 80

Eagle Dream 81

Contents

When I came to the part which said
"a thousand eyes observe,
a thousand ears hear all,
a thousands hands help and
support living beings everywhere"
I started to shake and tremble.

MARTY'S JOURNAL

WHEN newcomers come to Gold Mountain Dhyana Monastery in San Francisco and encounter the teaching and practice of the genuine Buddhadharma, it is not only unfamiliar sights and sounds that they are likely to experience. Unusual events are likely to take place within themselves. Sometimes these inner responses happen gradually; in other newcomers, the responses are powerful and immediate and without any precedent in the present lifetime of those who experience them. In each case, whether intense or mild, gradual or sudden, the responses can lead to a turning to the good, a growth in vigor and peace of mind, and a resolve upon enlightenment.

This booklet describes the responses that one American experienced when he came to Gold Mountain in 1976. Marty (the name he took a year later when he became a Shramanera - a novice monk) relates his experience in his own words. The extraordinary events that followed his meeting with the Buddhadharma have subsequently ripened into a strong devotion to the Buddha's teaching and a vigorous practice which are evidence of progress in cultivation in past lives and are testimony to future success in his career in the Way.

Born in Wisconsin in 1946, Marty grew up in a closely-knit Catholic family; he and his three sisters benefited from a wholesome, stable upbringing. He describes his parents as sensitive, decent, happy adults who inspired their children to investigate the world of the mind. His early education was in a Catholic setting, with Catholic nuns and priests as teachers. As for his high-school career, it was outstanding; honor student, star athlete, student council president; he was already on his way to worldly success in professional society. But even then he made it clear that unquestioning acceptance of the ordinary road was not to be his destiny; after high-school he almost entered noviate training under the Christian Brothers, only changing his mind at the last minute.

At the University of Wisconsin, Marty earned a B.A. and an M.A. in History and worn a Ford Foundation Fellowship for further graduate studies. While a student he began to experience with alternative lifestyles and alternate realities. He became proficient in martial arts (he traveled in Japan and Korea and earned the black belt in Korean karate), and offered his time and compassion as a visitor and counselor for the mentally ill and for emotionally disturbed children.

Marty dissatisfaction with the surface of life and with its ordinary pursuits led finally to a major change. His decisions to abandon his graduate studies and to dissolve his marriage of eight years reflected the depth of his need to discover the source of his own thoughts and to know the reasons behind the suffering he saw in the world. Increasing restlessness moved him to fast motorcycle rides, backpacking trips alone in the mountains, and other dangerous experiments. "I death-tripped for a time," he writes, "pushing myself closer and closer to the edge of sanity and reality. I was trying to reduce my ego and find my true self-nature at any cost. Thank goodness I had the sense to stop this self-destructive nonsense before I did any permanent damage to my body."

In 1975 and 1976, Marty lived in Berkeley, where he taught Tai Chi Ch'uan at the Wen Wu School and worked in a day-care center. An announcement of a Great Compassion Mantra recitation session drew him to Gold Mountain Monastery, and his career of cultivation of the Way in this life began. He became a disciple of the Venerable Master Hsuan Hua on the fifth day of the recitation session.

During the next year, Marty cultivation at home became regular and solid. He rose at five each morning, chanted morning recitation, sat in Chan meditation for an hour, practiced Tai Chi Ch'uan, followed by an hour of standing meditation. After ten months of cultivation as a Buddhist layman, he took the ten major and forty-eight minor Bodhisattva Precepts and made new vows to aid his cultivation. In April of 1977, he moved into Gold Mountain Monastery in preparation for the fulfillment of his vow to accompany, aid, and protect Bhikshu Heng Sure on Three Step One Bow pilgrimage from Los Angeles to the City of Ten Thousand Buddhas, 110 miles north San Francisco. The journey began May 7, 1977.

Marty was granted permission to enter monastic life. His head was shaved, and he received the ten vows of a novice monk. His name became Heng Chau.

"At a certain point," he writes, "I realized that there is nothing else worth doing in the world besides cultivating one's own wisdom and telling others about the Buddhadharma. America is ripe for Buddhism. We need its principles and its emphasis on morality, patience, and hard work. We Americans can no longer look outside for peace and happiness. We have reached the limits or our external expansion. It is now time to listen to the practice the principles of the Buddhadharma, to turn our energy inward, and to discover that the search for paradise that has always brought people to America ends ultimately in the discovery and the purification of one's own mind."

DECISION TO GO TO
GOLD MOUNTAIN

I HAD just returned to the t'ai chi studio after an hour of stand-meditation in a nearby field. While drinking a cup of tea, I noticed and announcement brochure for a Great Compassion Mantra Recitation Session at San Francisco's Gold Mountain Monastery. Intrigued by the language of the brochure, I read on. When I came to the part which said "a thousand eyes observe, a thousand ears hear all, a thousands hands help and support living beings everywhere" I started to shake and tremble. It felt like shivers, but all over, the kind that make your nose and eyes burn and sting just before tears come. Surprised and thrown off a bit, I decided to read it again. Same thing at the exact same lines. It happened three times in succession - shivers, shaking, and nearly tears. I decided to attend the session, knowing nothing of sitting meditation, chanting, Ch'an, and despite the strange and austere-looking monks and nuns in the photos. All that week before the session those lines from the brochure stuck in my mind. I found myself unconsciously hearing them and consciously echoing them.

GREAT COMPASSION SESSION

April 9, 1976

THE DAY I had scheduled to leave for Gold Mountain, three women friends (including my former wife) call with invitations for events happening the same time. I turn them down, but wonder at the coincidence. I arrive at the Monastery and balk - afraid to go in. See weird-looking, shaven-headed Sangha members and the stark simplicity of the building) a converted mattress factory in the heart of the Mission district). I remember the shaking while reading the announcement and I enter the door and sign in. Almost immediately the deja vus begin. First, I experience them with the people there, and then with the colors, the ceremonies, the smells, and so forth. I feel thrust out on a limb over an abyss and yet also at home, familiar.

April 10, 1976

See shining blue lotus flower while meditating after chanting. Resist all the bowing, especially to the Abbot. Seems too guru-ish and acquiescent.

April 12, 1976

Sutra lecture. I feel as if the Abbot is talking directly to me. The lecture and the commentary expose my very thoughts and they suit my present situation to a tee. See the light, bow to the Abbot. Feel relieved, disarmed.

<u>Specifics</u>: As I sat listening to the lecture on the *Avatamsaka Sutra*, the Abbot added to his commentary words to this effect: "Some people come to Buddhism with the misconception that they are enlightened already. Or that their knowledge and learning place them above everyone else. They come to the Way-Place looking to be recognized, honored, placed on a pedestal. They are full of themselves; looking to wear a high hat, or to be crowned with a high hat. How pitiful! They come to a mountain of jewels, but leave empty-handed. I will tell you: arrogance is an obstacle; it's like a poison. You are so full of self that there's no room for any Dharma to enter. Hah! and worst of all one who is afflicted with arrogance thinks 'I alone am pure and blameless.'"

When the Abbot spoke these words, I felt extremely self-conscious and uncomfortable, as if he were talking right to me. Yet, how could this be? He did not even no me; we had never talked, and only met a few days ago. Then I realized that I had met a person who knew me better than I knew myself. I was in fact arrogant, and never saw it, never acknowledged it. His words penetrated right to my heart. I felt both ashamed and strangely freed. I thought to myself, "Anyone who can know me better and truer than I know myself, I could bow to," even though I resisted bowing from the very moment I entered the door of the monastery. So, after the lecture ended and everyone was paying their respects to the Abbot as he sat in a chair in the back of hall, I slipped in behind the last people in the rear (so as not to be noticed by the Abbot) and bowed three times. Suddenly the Abbot craned his neck to look at me directly with a strangely kind and ironic smile. "How does it feel?" he asked. "Do you remember? I am sure I blushed, and suddenly found myself without words.

DECISION TO TAKE REFUGE

April 15, 1976

DEJA VUS stronger now, more frequent and longer lasting. While bowing to the Buddhas in what seems an incredibly drawn-out and boring ritual, an ineffable thing happens: in the space of a very few minutes my entire life reels by - flashes before me. Every event, every person, every trauma, decision, relationship, place, noise, and chance acquaintance passes in vivid, detailed clarity. I see my life and understand it totally, without a shadow of question and without effort. And most inconceivably, it all leads right to the present, to where I am bowing on this cushion, on this day, in Gold Mountain Monastery. I am right where I am supposed to be, right where I had to be. I am back without having ever left. It felt like a timeless, unending deja vu, only clearer, more complete, with no vagueness. It all made sense. It felt like the kids' game of groping around a dark room and trying to tell by textures, size, and location what the objects in the room are. Then after guessing, someone switches on the light and Oh, of course! That's what it was! And that was the clock, that was the pillow, the broom; now I see. The experience is difficult to express.

The Abbot had been walking around the assembly and was now seated in his chair in the rear of the Buddhahall. Bhikshus Heng Kuan and Heng Sure where talking with him. I went back to speak with the Abbot because that was the only thing that felt right to do. He was the only person whom I wanted to try to tell about my experience. I could barely talk. I felt tall choked-up, embarrassed and totally unhinged. I felt fearless, without thought or concern. My senses perceived everything vividly, everything was alive and yet ethereal, without substance or finality. Even the pattern on the floor title and the rip in the bowing cushion made sense. I finally managed to say that I wanted to take refuge in the Triple Jewel - to become a disciple. All the Abbot did was to smile and say, "Try your best."

I then went upstairs to my room and sat on the edge of the bed. I began to cry uncontrollably, crying like I have never cried before or since. Why cry when I felt so filled with joy? Partly it was a feeling of joy because everything was so pure and clear, with no end and no beginning. There were no walls, no limits, and no confusion, no past and no future. But it was also a feeling of shame for all the stupid and hateful energies I had set in motion in the past. In part I felt gratitude for all the countless numbers of people who were sacrificing for me, who were extending kindness to me, protecting me and teaching me. How could I even begin to repay their kindness? I felt overwhelming feelings of selfishness, inadequacy, and guilt. Finally I cried tears of fear and sadness which were prompted by a vision of what was to come. And over all, I felt a pure and peaceful emptiness. I felt at home and nowhere.

During the next chanting period, three "dreams" which I had dreamt before I had heard of Gold Mountain returned to mind with an extraordinary resonance. And this time, they made sense. The order in which the dreams occurred, the people in the dreams, the images, and the dialogue of the dreams all fell into place. While I walked and chanted in the session each dream recurred with vivid succession. Each dream displaced a variety of riddles and added another non-ordinary dimension to my Gold Mountain experience. The dreams all took on a rich spiritual meaning and direction. Suddenly I understood and absorbed the message of the dreams. Some sort of dam had burst within my mind. The water, stiff and frozen behind the dam was now running wild and fast.

DREAM NUMBER ONE

THIS dream occurred following a prolonged illness I endured after nearly dying in Death Valley on a camping trip. The time was exactly one year before (the full moon of the third lunar month). In fact it was not really a dream. I actually left my body and traveled through time and space, somewhere to rolling, arid, desert mesa. Two non-Western men (Anglo-Spanish-Indian) led me to a low hill, and told me to lie down. They said that I would lapse into a sleep-like state and that when I woke up, "everything would be all right." They said that I would "know" - there would be no more problems or any need of further help - I would know clearly what to do. When I awakened on the hill the two men were gone. I was quite alone out in the middle of nowhere. Yet everything was different. In my lower abdomen, around the navel, there was a glowing, radiant, silver-white ball of light about the size of a bowling ball. As soon as I grew aware of the light within me I no longer felt isolated or hesitant. I immediately began to walk to the southwest or to the southeast. I knew before I arrived that I would find a small town. I knew who the inhabitants were and what language they spoke before I saw or heard them; I could tell friends from enemies, right choices from wrong choices, all at a glance. No action required conscious thought or effort. All I had to do was accord with conditions and conditions were manifestly, obviously evident. I had no difficulties with communication even though I could not speak or understand the language of the town. This fact was unimportant. If I really needed to get through I could do it with my eyes or in one case, by gently but decisively placing my hand on someone's lower stomach.

This "dream" ended as someone walked past me while reciting lines from a poem about birth and death. The person was perplexed by the poem. I recognized the lines and their meaning as clearly as if I had written them myself. Later, when "I" returned to my sleeping body I felt totally disoriented. The feeling of well being and the silver ball of light, the effortless seeing and the feeling of peace were all still with me. But when I returned to the world I could no longer relate to the world or to the people whom I "knew". Reality was still the same, but different - it now felt transparent, gossamer-like.

Especially I did not know the identity of the body called "me" and how it related to the new and much different "me" of the desert vision. The people and things around me were as unfamiliar and as unimportant now as the environment around the desert village had been in my vision. I still could feel the silver-white light inside of me and I still felt as if it were guiding me. I barely made it through those first days back and nothing has ever been as before since that experience. Layer upon layer, the world I knew peeled away.

DREAM NUMBER TWO

I AM climbing and hiking along a narrow, rocky trail in a desolate and craggy mountain region. I am wearing a small pack and ascending long switchbacks. I am alone. I was not clear where I am going or why. Even though it is quiet and uninhabited, a sense of imminent danger and encounter pervades. At one point I see a large man just ahead (he is giant-sized) and he is crouching behind a rock. He has a rifle and he is waiting in the brush for me. I am not certain why, but it seems that he is waiting for vengeance for something that I did to him or to someone close to him in the past. As the man is about to aim his rifle, suddenly an indistinct figure (a guide) appears and leads me into a cave on the side of the mountain. The entrance is small and inside, the ceiling is low. My pack is an encumbrance, an obstacle to free movement. There is a strange ritual or ceremony in progress in the cave. There is chanting, gesturing, fires and movement. The ceremony is conducted almost exclusively by a leaderless group of women. They bear no particular individual characteristics. They help me remove my pack. There is a fire and water cleansing and something involving ashes takes place. Fully cleansed and with my head partially shaved I am led out of the cave. The women remain inside. They seem together, and strong and sure of their actions and their roles. They seem at peace within the cave.

Outside it is very clear and light. There is a

group of men, all with shaven heads. My head
too is now completely shaven. I become aware
of an older man who is set apart from the rest
and whose head is also shaven. At this point the
sniper withdraws from the scene. The old man
tells me something but he does not
communicate with words. He might be Asian
or Indian and he appears quite different. He
points to a distant mountain range. Although I
hadn't seen it before I entered the cave, this
range of mountains partially surrounded me
while I hiked. The mountains resemble a series
of steep cones or spires (approximately seven of
them). The man tells me that I must climb them
- alone. Even though I will have a guide his
presence will be discreet and indirectly
supportive. I learn that all the legwork and all
the effort of the ascend will be done by me alone.
The guide will be always visible but he will be

flanking me and he will be seen from the corner of my eye, a peripheral shadow. The guide will keep me on the right track but he will not assist me directly as he would if we were mountain climbing together.

The old man is kind but serious, straightforward and not superfluous. He says the climb is not impossible, but it is not easy, either. One of the spires I will climb has unknown quality about it. The old man points it out and explains that this particular mountain will be my real test. There are words written on the backside of the mountain. If I don't interpret and handle the situation correctly then I will fall. I won't be seriously hurt, nor fall all the way back to where I began. I'll simply have to repeat the climb until I do it right.

The old man's chest and torso are bare to partially covered. The mountain is a strange admixture of colors: purple, gold, red; it is magnetic and imposing.

DREAM NUMBER THREE

I AM flying in a makeshift airplane, as I have done many times before. My T'ai Chi teacher is sitting in the second cockpit behind me. I enjoy the sensation of flight but until now I could never rise much higher than the trees or the tangle of the power lines. This time, however, we pull the throttle and climb almost straight up, soaring above the wires, trees, and clouds. The T'ai Chi teacher bails out and says, "You're on your own, this is as far as I go!" Soon the atmosphere changes in texture and in quality. It becomes a blend of heavy air and light water. The plane has fallen behind and I'm floating and swimming in a semi-slow-motion suspension. There is little gravity, and a buoyant sensation, and breathing is no problem. The air is unimaginably pure and sweet. Everything I encounter is floating along unattached, serenely and quietly. There is no up or down, no top or bottom. I have no sense of when it all began or where I came in.

The diving fin on my foot and the obviously useless parachute, which is dangling on my back, seem ridiculous, comic. Yet they do provide a false sense of security they are there just in case. The objects that float near me or that I approach all hold fascination and mystery. Each is outlined in pristine relief of rare colors and subtle hues. I feel that I could explore this realm endlessly.

The diving fin falls off and floats away, landing on some aquatic plants. I retrieve it and laugh at myself for clinging to it like a child clings to a security blanket. Suddenly I find myself being inexorably drawn down a tunnel-like tube of plants. At the end of the tunnel there in an opening to another world, a world less blissful and serene than the present one. The end of the tunnel in my floating "heaven" is the entrance to a cave. The cave opens into the world I'm moving toward. Two men climb up along a trail outside the cave's mouth. I resist being discharged into the other world but I have no control. For some uncertain reason, perhaps due to fear or perhaps in order to alert or to frighten the men outside the cave, I yell out just before and then again while being discharged. I awake abruptly.

AFTER THE SESSION

THERE were other dreams, deja vus, and similar experiences that continued to happen whenever I was inside Gold Mountain following that week of the Great Compassion Session. None of them were as starling, as mind-blowing, as intensely inclusive as the experiences of the first week. What happened after the session seemed by comparison to be rather ordinary, as extraordinary things go.

On several occasions I went to the Monastery or to attend a session feeling troubled about a particular question. While meditating or while in the presence of the Ven. Abbot, the answer to the question would come to me. Most often the answer would appear when I would recall a dream or a previous deva-vu experience. It was as if the answers anticipated the questions. The journey would describe a return, a remembering process.

Throughout the whole of one Ch'an session I was plagued by a personal problem and I kept hoping for a solution to appear. The longer I struggled with the question, the longer and the more frustrating became the sitting periods of the session. The last period of the session arrived and I still had no answer. I decided to give up searching and simply concentrate on my inner recitation. I forgot my pain and I forgot my question. Just then the Abbot happened to walk past, apparently on an inspection tour around the Ch'an Hall. As he passed by there was a flash of blue light, followed by a vision of part of an old dream. The dream clearly pointed to my question and resolved it. The bell sounded and the session was over.

On another occasion I sat brooding on a stool in the kitchen just before the final sitting period of a Great Compassion Mantra session. I was brooding about how I was ever going to handle all my new changes in life-style and new disruptions in familiar patterns that would result from the experiences of this session. The Ven. Abbot casually strolled into the kitchen, circled once around my stool, looked at my head above my eyes and left without saying a word. Suddenly my head cleared and the words "hard work and patience" popped into consciousness. The heaviness dissipated. The words proved to be valuable advice.

CEREMONY FOR TAKING
THE DEAD ACROSS

(August 10, 1973)

I HAVE never attended such a ceremony; I was a little in awe of it, a little skeptical, but very mindful of the people whom I had come to represent. While chanting and bowing and holding in mind the names of the dead friends and relatives, I lost myself. As we started to chant the mantra for sending the dead off to rebirth in the Western Land of Ultimate Bliss, a noticeable change took place. I felt wide-open, empathetic, and touched by sadness and pity. The Ven. Abbot had come downstairs and was standing in the back of the hall. We began to circumambulate the hall while chanting the mantra. Each time I passed near the Abbot, feelings of compassion would surge inside, rise up and flood me. After the second or third pass in front of the Ven. Abbot, tears were trickling down my face. I suppressed them because I felt slightly embarrassed to be crying. Each subsequent pass before the Master, however, brought another wave of sympathy and more tears. This experience continued until the name-plaques of the dead were burned and the ceremony was ended. This was Ullambana, "the Buddha's happy day".

DREAM OF MY GRANDFATHER

I HAVE always been close to and fond of my grandfather; we spent much time together while I was growing up and he was one of my teachers. I was the last person he recognized from his deathbed. Our names are the same and our birth dates are within days of each other. I represented him at the Ullambana ceremony, the ceremony for taking the dead across. Some time after the ceremony I visited my grandfather in a dream. He was serene but quite animated. The shadows and marks of stress and strain during his life were all gone; he bore no sign of his responsibilities and burdens. He looked venerable but still young. I remember in particular how light-hearted he seemed, almost frivolous.

The location of the dream was indistinct but the air was clean and light, the colors were bright, and it seemed spacious and liberating. His attitude towards me was warm and instructive; he advised me directly on an issue that had been troubling me. His advice and his warning to me were simple and direct. The truth of his words hit home immediately. He told me to seek the highest path and to be sure not to settle for anything less. He said that nothing was more true, nothing more important than that. That was it. As ever, he needed to say just a few words and we both knew the rest. As the dream faded, my grandfather was reciting a mantra. I didn't recognize what mantra it was.

THE "GHOST" IN THE HOUSE

GINNY (Kuo Chieh) and I have set aside a small room for meditation. We erected an altar with images of Buddhas and Bodhisattvas, a pot for incense, flowers, and the rest. One day Ginny claimed that she was being bothered during her meditation by a strange heavy breathing which seemed to come from behind her. I had never heard the noise; of course I was skeptical. We investigated all the possible "reasonable" explanations and discovered nothing.

A few days later while meditating, I also heard the noise. It was the distinct and somewhat forced breathing of an older person who is sick or whose lungs are congested. It was located directly behind me and very close. I didn't look around because my curiosity is weaker than my intuitive caution. I simply ignored it and tried not to be moved by panic or distracted in the least. But I was moved. I had just memorized the first 26 lines of the Shurangama Mantra, so the next day, when the breathing began again, I tried reciting the mantra aloud. Halfway through the second recitation of the first 26 lines, the breathing disappeared and it has never returned since then.

DREAMS AND MAGIC SPELLS

THERE have been many times when I have woken from dreams to find myself reciting mantras or calling out to Buddhas and Bodhisattvas. I have awakened in a sweat after disturbing or threatening dreams and discovered that I was reciting. After I decided to memorize the Shurangama Mantra a very interesting dream occurred. In this dream an other worldly human being approached me. He was human but strange looking and threatening. From some reason he wanted me to join in a black-magic ritual that was taking place nearby. His influence was dark and cold and he was reciting a mantra on beads. His aura field was very yin and unhealthy. For some reason I didn't flee in panic but sat down in the lotus posture and recited what I knew of the Shurangama Mantra.

Almost immediately I felt enclosed in a warm, glowing, semi-transparent tent of light. Although the dark being could see me, and although I was aware of his presence just outside of my protective clearing, something was encircling me and he could not touch me. Eventually, he turned away and rejoined the bizarre ritual beyong. It was a group of entranced, zombie-like people; their bodies were a sickly, bluish-gray color and they mechanically embraced each other. Their embrace sealed an understanding between them, a malevolent affinity.

I stood up and immediately found myself

out-of-doors, preparing to leave on a journey. I was in the company of Ginny and a Bhikshu from Gold Mountain. It was the same Bhikshu who first told me of the Shurangama Mantra and encouraged me to cultivate it.

VOWS

AT THE beginning of an Amitabha Recitation
session I took a vow of silence. I intended to
begin the same evening; I wished to keep silence
from the start of my stay at the monastery. But,
seeing some friends in the hallway, I broke the
vow and settled into a lively and totally useless
discussion in the back of the Buddhahall
following the evening ceremonies. While we
were chattering away, the Abbot came
downstairs and walked directly over to the group
of us and sternly said, "Who gave you permission
to break the rules? Who said that you could
talk?" I knew immediately upon hearing him

coming down the stairs that I had blown it. I felt like a reprimanded adolescent...I was caught being the child I used to be.

Shortly after that I made a vow to sleep no more than six hours a night. I wanted to restrict my laziness; I needed more time to cultivate. I decided to begin the practice immediately even though it would be at least a week before I would make the vow "official" by announcing it before the Great Assembly at Gold Mountain. That morning the alarm rang after six hours of sleep. I was in the middle of a fascinating dream and I said to myself, "Well, you haven't officially made the vow and it won't really matter this one time whether you get up or not..." I quickly rationalized myself back to sleep.

But right in the middle of the pleasant dream the scene abruptly switched to Gold Mountain Monastery. There was a session in progress in my dream. Instead of meditating I was up on the second floor socializing. Just then, the Ven. Abbot came walking up the stairs. Like a sneaky kid caught with his hand in the cookie jar, I quickly slapped my legs into lotus position and tried to appear as if I had been absorbed in meditation. Nobody was fooled. I started awake from the dream and got up to do morning chanting and meditation.

PRECEPTS...."RIGHT ON TIME."

BEFORE taking the precepts I held the common misconception that I should wait until I could hold them before going through the ceremony. I sincerely desired to receive the precepts, however, and I didn't stand behind this excuse; rather, I went ahead and held the precepts in my daily life. After a few months of following a precepted life-style I noticed changes for the better in my behavior and in my attitudes and I decided to sign up for the five and the eight lay precepts. For various reasons, most of them nothing more than false-thinking and self-deception, I was convinced that I had to take

47

the precepts at a certain time, that is to say within a certain month. I became attached to the timing and the immediacy of taking the precepts at this specific time. Amazingly enough, there was a precept-transmission ceremony scheduled for that very weekend. I was elated and ecstatic, lost in my narrow vision of self. I thought, "What a cultivator I must be…..such a coincidence! How auspicious!"

Instead of going to the City of Ten Thousand Buddhas that weekend as I had originally planned, (the Ven. Abbot was accompanying a small group of disciples to the City for a tour and a lecture), I decided to lay back and indulge in a final fling of having my cake and eating it too. "After all," I thought, "I'm clearly grooving right along – I'm 'right on time'."

The precepts were to be transmitted on a Sunday at Gold Mountain after the sutra lecture. In a dream Saturday night I found myself in Ukiah with the Abbot and his party. (Although I had not yet been to the City of Ten Thousand Buddhas, when I actually did visit I found it to be identical with the place I saw in this dream). Everyone was preparing for an important ceremony but I was constantly wandering off and getting lost. When the group was inside chanting I was out taking a stroll. I never did figure out what was happening, but I knew that I was missing it. Finally, after I did manage to catch up with the group, the ceremony was over. The Abbot slowly turned to me and said, "Well, have a good one."

I awoke from the dream feeling a little bewildered, but shrugged off the dream and went through Sunday as planned. I slept in, ate a leisurely breakfast at a restaurant, took a nap and sauntered over to the monastery "right on time". I had had a "good one".

When I entered the monastery door, all the Sangha members I had seen in my dream the night before were congregating near the High Seat. Incense filled the hall. A young layman came up to me and said innocently, "You should have come earlier, you could have seen the precept ceremony." I felt as if the floor had given way. I was spinning in a void. I could not contain my shocked disbelief and disappointment. I had missed precepts! They had been transmitted after the <u>afternoon</u> sutra lecture. Since I had never been there on a Sunday afternoon, I had assumed the lecture was in the evening. If I had gone to Ukiah, of course, I would have been "right on time".

My emotions flashed from self-pity to anger, and then to despair. I thought, "Nobody cares. I'll leave. What's the use? I'll stop cultivating."

It wasn't until the evening bowing ceremony which follows the lecture that I stopped spinning and got myself together. I understood how I had engineered the entire situation through my stupid ego and through my attachments. This was the source of my misery. I resolved to take the precepts when they were offered the next time around.

For some reason the Ven. Abbot happened to be in the kitchen that evening after the bowing. I went into the kitchen to bow to him in repentance and in gratitude for the shake-up and the lesson I had received. As I approached, Ginny came up to me and said, "Did you hear?" "Hear what?" "The Abbot says that you can take the precepts in a couple of days at the Ullambana ceremony." I was spinning again. "He heard that you were unhappy because you missed them today, so he said that you could take them Tuesday, because he doesn't want you to be unhappy," she explained. More spinning, more lessons.

I'm never where I think I am in this cultivation of the Way. Always on the edge. That's Gold Mountain—there's lots of rope and spaces to climb up out of one's afflictions or stupidity or to hang oneself with. I bowed to the Abbot. He seemed thoroughly unmoved, amused, and understanding. "Try your best!" he said.

CH'AN SESSION

If you want to be filial in one hundred ways,
First you must learn to cultivate the Way.

Ch'an Master Hua

MY FIRST Ch'an session was all surprises. I didn't know what to expect. I had apprehensions and I feared the unknown. Instead of the mysterious mental and physical terror I anticipated the session was just a lot of quite, hard work and a renewing, solitary encounter. It was a lot like backpacking alone or the feeling that follows a crying session that has been restrained for too long. After each sitting period, after struggling with my aching body and cluttered head came an expansive calm and cleaned-out emptiness (alone, all-one). Towards the end of the session the pain in my legs and hips either dissipated or else I forgot to notice it. The frenetic dribble of my mind, like my body, exhausted itself and let go. Suddenly I found myself experiencing all these clear, resonant flashes of my parents.

Subtly and comprehensively I realized my inconceivable debt to my parents. They effortlessly lived and embodied a purity and a selflessness that I was only now beginning to discover. Their wisdom and compassion, their lack of deviousness came naturally. The compassion and artlessness I showed was awkward and self-conscious. I usually though before I felt. And I had to "work on" remembering how to feel. They moved truly from their hearts. I reaped all the benefits of living with such remarkable people, oblivious to my good fortune and certainly doing little to repay or to reciprocate their kindness.

Whatever spiritual roots and conditions I had came through them. My base of spiritual and physical strength and faith I owed to them as well. Somehow because of my parents, just by being who they are, I intuitively knew that enlightenment wasn't a pipe dream. They gave the concept substance, put my originally face (nature) within reach. I could see it in them, so I could eventually find it too. Every living being could and would in time lay it down and return home.

If I tried to examine this logically, to explain this "understanding," my head could not expand to hold it. But right then, emptied and exhausted, for a few fleeting moments something inside me could hold it. In my "heart" I knew my parents were the source and the inspiration of an urge to plunge in deeper. Shortly after this experience I took the lay precepts.

CH'AN SESSION BRAT

THIS entire Ch'an session was painful. Distractions and false-thinking tossed me around like a stick in a pounding surf. I couldn't get on top of it. Even though I wasn't talking, my mind and my eyes blabbered incessantly. I felt like a colander—my energy flowed out by over-eating, by scrutinizing and finding faults in others. Giving in to the slightest pain, I was constantly crossing and uncrossing my legs. I anticipated each bell ending the hour sitting period a good half-hour before it rang.

During the first sit after lunch I could barely

stay awake. I must have switched my legs two or three times. Finally, I had had it. I resolved to strap my legs into lotus and to hold the Great Compassion Mantra with a mind and a body that did not move for the next hour. Dead set as I was, difficulties seemed to increase. For some reason I felt a presence on my left side, just on the edge of peripheral vision. It was the source of all my turbulence. By sitting still I was able to locate it and to bring it into sharper focus. I continued to recite. Then without turning my body or my head, I sharply turned my mind. Don't ask me how I did it, I never did anything like it before. I didn't think about it, I just did it, it just happened. I turned my mind and caught it!

It looked like an ugly little brat of a kind— an unruly and out-of-control child. All throughout the session this little brat had been taunting and hazing me. When I would try to catch or to identify him he would split away. Only frustration and an on-edge distraction remained. But caught off guard, this time the brat was cornered and trapped. My huge anger and hatred, once I actually caught and inspected my tormentor up close, turned to pity and understanding. It was just a frightened little kid making all the fuss. A little problem child, insecure, and fueled with a lot of fire and a big ego. Hardly the bete noir I had imagined.

Without words, a peace and a kind of understanding friendship was reached. The Great Compassion Mantra brought us together and kept us apart. Subdued, we returned to the session. We both sat in a quiet mindfulness the rest of the week.

BODHISATTVA PRECEPTS

FOR THREE consecutive nights before and after receiving the Bodhisattva precepts I experienced vivid dreams about the Sangha at Gold Mountain. The first took place in a dense fog on hilly terrain. I was looking for something or for someone, but I couldn't penetrate the thick mist. I wanted to do T'ai Chi on the road, but there wasn't a road. I started to do a set on the level top of a hill. In the distance, coming through the fog, I heard a mantra being chanted in chugging-train rhythm. Two Bhikshunis (nuns) emerged, walking tandem and purposefully along a road. The road passed right in front of me. I could not see it until the nuns defined it with their erect procession and chanting. Later, half-submerged in a stream, I found myself sharing a huge, long string of recitation beads with a group of left-home and lay disciples. The water was washing over us as we recited in unison.

The next night there was something like a dress-rehearsal involving Sangha members, myself, and a ritual. I was following them but I was not sure of my role or of the purpose of the ritual. Large wooden tubs, like Japanese <u>ofuro</u> baths, were in a hall. We were cleaning and arranging them, and later we practiced getting in and out of them.

The last dream occurred on the same night as the precept transmission ceremony. The tubs from the dream of the previous night were set in the same halls and now they were filled with water. In the dream, a solemn ritual was in progress and the tubs were vessels for a ritual bathing.

(Flashback) Before coming to Gold Mountain I was taking a Japanese bath alone, outside. After a long submersion I surfaced. Suddenly I felt this strong urge to shave my head. It felt really strange. That same week during a massage, some switch or some trigger connected and I vividly recall being inside my mother's womb. I can hear voices of my parents outside. I do not know what they are saying but I note how "outside" my father's voice sounds and how "inside" my mother's voice reverberates.

This dream has a similar feel to the dream I dreamt in April when I saw a ceremony inside a cave. The hall was illuminated with a soft, yellow-gold light. The same Sangha members were involved in the ceremonies, participating and assisting. I was in one of the tubs.

AMITABHA SESSION

I TOOK a vow of silence and fasted the last two days of the session. I had to leave in the middle of the session to go to work. That day was full of all sorts of small karmic obstacles (Vespa motorscooter breakdown, truck problems, other frustrations). I have just finished reading the Vajra Sutra (published by BTTS). It has profound effect on me. I find the sutra ultimately truthful and it provides a kind of life-saving nourishment. At the same time there is a sense of "losing my mind" and losing my identity and this sense stirs up my fears and my fascination.

During the last sitting period of the session I stood up in meditation in the back of the Buddhahall. When I do standing meditation at that spot in the Gold Mountain Buddhahall I stare at the image of Shakyamuni Buddha which sits behind the High Seat, the Ven. Abbot's lecture podium. Near the end of this period I felt a tingling sensation on the top of my head. It felt like a small bug was crawling there. The stone-jewel in the Buddha's forehead seemed to sparkle.

The Ven. Abbot's lecture followed. The stark luminous wisdom of his words struck me as never before. He talked about the Shurangama Mantra and the role of scholars in hastening the "Dharma-ending Age". I made connections and saw things in my own life and in my academic career, which now made sense at last. Unresolved issues and questions finally untangled themselves.

Doubts and alternatives which I had never been able to synthesize or to verbalize suddenly fell into place. I realized that the many years I had spent stumbling around in a blind and cynical head-trip had confused me, had led me to throw out the baby with the bath water, as far as my education was concerned. The answers had been there all along, right before my eyes and before my heart. The Abbot's words shone. I was absorbed. The hall was alive and bathed in a soft yellow-gold light.

Later that night back in Berkeley I was jolted out of bed by an earthquake. It was the hardest of a series of mild tremors that continued to shake for several days. Instinctively I went to our apartment's altar room and made an incense offering and then recited mantras. While chanting, I had a total, gut-level experience. I realized the impermanence and the thread-like nature of this life. I realized the illusion of the "solid earth". At that moment nothing was more important or more real than cultivating real gung fu, genuine spiritual accomplishment that could help me and help others to face the ultimate issue: the journey "from cradle to grave". Time was an indulgence, something that I clung to when I wanted to drift along lazily, trying to pretend that I could avoid the ultimate showdown with death. I was waiting, as the verse says: "Like a fish in evaporating water…"

I realized that I wished to have my cake and eat it too. With my practices of T'ai Chi Ch'uan, meditation sessions, and holding precepts, I would work towards a state of purity in body, mouth, and mind, a state of "no-outflows", no energy leaks. Yet despite this resolute cultivation I was in the habit of running out at every chance and wasting my energies on empty diversions. My mind filled with fragments of verses and watchwords: true motion in stillness is two steps forward, two steps back, and it all equals foursteps nowhere; my favorite phrase from childhood: "take me time, take me time," not much had really changed since then; "I am still young….the best years of my life….lots of time left, lots of time….." It all shook that night.

EARTHQUAKE DREAM

RETURNING to bed after the earthquake on the night of the Amitabha Session's wind-up, I had the following dream: I saw the same sequence of events as I had actually experienced hours earlier; only in the dream, the earthquake registered a few points higher on the Richter scale. Instead of mild jolts, it meant disaster. I could hear screaming and wailing, I heard the moans of friends and neighbors who were thrown about by explosions or crushed beneath buildings and walls that twisted and collapsed. The suffering and the pain I felt while helplessly watching other people within and dying on all sides was beyond words. It was an uncontrollable nightmare in slow-motion.

There was no place to run for safety, nowhere to hide. Each ripping, rippling shrug of the earth impassively rolled on, immune and oblivious to the terror and the supplication of the human victims. It was like pleading with the ocean to stop the waves. I remember feeling totally helpless and powerless to stop the disaster or even to cope with myself and my reaction to it. It was like a similar time a few years earlier when I was surrounded by bears while camping in the Sierra Mountains. I was alone; in fact, I was miles from the nearest human aid and it was midnight on a moonless, black night. The presence of the bears popped all my illusions of power and I lost the fantasy of youthful immortality. These comforting dreams exploded like cheap balloons.

That night in the Sierras and now with the earthquake I realized that most of my thoughts and habits were based on a foundation of make-believe. They were empty, like the fearful prattling of children spooked by the dark. I realized that my understanding of reality is based upon the mirage of self-importance and power. This mirage thrives on fear and ignorance: the fear of facing the unknown, and the ignorance of ultimate principles. The ignorance feeds the fear, the fear bolsters the ignorance, and they both inflate the illusion-balloons.

At this point in my dream I saw the Master. He dwelt in the middle of a bright and expansive clearing. I had to get to him and to bring as many people along with me as I could. But the roads to the clearing were washed out and there were human obstacles as well: selfish, insensitive, dreamy people were teamed with demonic beings who wanted to continue the ruin and the suffering I witnessed in my dream.

When I awoke I quickly looked outside. Houses and streets were still intact. I could hear children playing. People who lived across the road were returning from market with bags full of groceries. In short, everything was fine. Yet something in me had changed. My world had stopped. These questions came to mind: When was I truly awake and when was I more asleep? Which state was real and which state was more unreal – the dream-state or the waking-state? Clearer now, I resolved to myself that it was now time to stop delaying; it was time to tighten the loose ends of my life, time to plug the leaks, and time to get on with the business of cultivation for real.

EARTHQUAKE VOWS

THAT morning I made the following vows:

Before all the Buddhas and Bodhisattvas of the ten directions and the three periods of time, before the Venerable Master and the fourfold assembly, I, Disciple Kuo T'ing, make these vows.

To repay the kindness of my parents, my teachers, and the Venerable Master, I vow to cut off attachments and marks of self, to constantly maintain a resolve for Bodhi, to study all Dharma-doors, and to transfer any merit and virtue to the entire family of living beings.

I vow to recite the Great Compassion Mantra 108 times daily.

I vow never to sleep while sitting in meditation.

I vow to memorize and recite the Shurangama Mantra daily.

I further resolve to practice the following:

To attend more sutra lectures regularly so as to better understand and to better speak the Buddhadharma.

To sleep no more than six hours a day

To vigorously hold and maintain the five and the eight lay precepts and the ten major and the forty-eight minor Bodhisattva precepts.

To recite and to study these precepts twice a month.

I further resolve to use whatever skills and strengths I have to maintain and to protect the Triple Jewel and to cultivate the Bodhisattva

Way with body, mouth, and mind.

I vow to cut off all false-thinking, outflows and attachments, especially of self, and to bring forth a vajra body and mind.

I vow that all vows will be fulfilled and that any merit and virtue will be transferred so that all living beings can end suffering and return to our original, awakened Buddha-nature.

FILIALITY

SINCE that first Ch'an session the conviction and the understanding of my debt to my parents deepened. I sought some way to repay them, but I could not find a way that satisfied. One evening in January, while circumambulating and chanting before the sutra lecture, my mind was peppered with memories and flashes of my parents. Like a slide-show I visualized a sequence of incidents which demonstrated their fineness, their quality. My consciousness was flooded with memories long forgotten, early and subtle imprints of their kindness and virtue. I tried to recite singlemindedly but the memories persisted. They had their own momentum and it was too late to block the channels.

As the Ven. Abbot descended the stairs to the Buddhahall I crossed directly below him. At the same moment I saw my parents in an unimaginable state. Their faces were radiant and smooth, clear and glowing with a peaceful energy. They were free of doubts, needs, and desires. They were fulfilled and they beamed indescribable smiles and calmness. I was moved to tears.

During the sutra lecture that followed, more pieces of the puzzle fell into place. How it all happened I do not understand. The lecture established an evenness of mind and a feeling of calm. A soothing order and clarity settled in my mind. I "knew" that in this life they were my parents. But who were my parents before this lifetime? Who will be my parents in the future? Who was I a parent to in past lives? In future lives? Friends and family in this lifetime could easily become parents, wives, or children in the next. It is likely that friends and kin in this life are the relatives and associates of lives past.

As I pondered this revelation, my familiar discriminations and tidy divisions of time and space gave way. I was not left with a feeling of isolation or of alienation, rather I had a profound sense of inclusion in a huge extended family. Everyone and everything was related. I realized that all of us came from, cared for and returned to the same pond. It was all the same. I felt a circle come to completion.

The lines that drew me to Gold Mountain, the lines of the Great Compassion Session brochure, "to help and support living beings everywhere", were somehow part of the circle.

No words could catch the mystery.

PT. REYES MANTRA

ON THE beach at Pt. Reyes as night falls and a heavy fog rolls in, Ginny and I both feel weird vibes and a threatening presence. I close my eyes and think of the Abbot. With eyes still closed I see to my left a circular wheel. I remember it from the Dharani Sutra, The 42 Hand section. For some reason I shape my right hand to hold the shape of the little golden wheel. I recite the Great Compassion Mantra and before long, everything feels better, like something has lifted and smoothed, calm.

EAGLE DREAM

OUT walking in an expansive forest with Joshua and Kevin (two children I was a "second father" to). The day is illuminated by a strange, dry light. We see a magnificent eagle gliding, soaring. It descends too low. Suddenly, smaller birds attack the eagle. They are flocks of hawks and they drive the eagle lower. He cannot maneuver through the trees – and I feel and immediate surge of compassion and empathy, and I rush over to help the eagle. When I arrive, the bird is still alive but it is dying. The top of its body, the torso, changes into a man's body. It looks directly at me and gives me a warning and a piece of advice. I cannot remember the words but my heart recalls the message: the eagle tried to return to a place it had outgrown. It had gone beyond and it tried to return to an inferior place. This was the cause of its death. The bird should have stayed in the higher regions where eagles belong; it was no longer a forest hawk. The other hawks resented it, feared and felt threatened by the eagle's return. I felt as if the eagle had sacrificed his life knowingly in order to make a point, in order to advise me.

Index

A

Abbot 15, 37, 75
Amitabha Session 68
anger 58
arrogance 16

B

bears 69
Bhikshu 44
black magic 43
Bodhisattva precepts 60
bowing 15
brat 58

C

cave dream 27
Ch'an session 35, 54, 57
compassion 37
concentration 35
crying 20, 38, 76
cultivation 71

D

dead souls 37
Death Valley dream 23
deja vu 14, 18
dream of City of 10,000 Buddhas 49
dreams 21, 43

E

eagle dream 79
earthquake 65
earthquake dream 68
earthquake vows 72
ego 51

F

family 77
flying dream 31
fog dream 60

G

golden wheel 78
grandfather dream 39
gratitude 20
Great Compassion Mantra 59, 72, 78
Great Compassion Session 34

H

habits 66, 69
hard work 36
hawks 80
heavy breathing 41

I

ignorance 70
impermanence 65

J

joy 20

K

knowledge 15

L

laziness 46

M

mantra 40, 60
meditation 63

P

parents 55, 56, 62, 72, 75, 76
patience 36
precepts 48, 73

R

rebirth mantra 37
recitation beads 60
ritual dream 61
rules 45

S

sacrifice 80
Sangha 60
Sangha members 14
see entire life 18
shame 20
Shurangama Mantra 42, 43, 44, 64, 72
silence 45
sleep 45, 73
sleep sitting up 72
sutra lectures 73

T

take refuge 20
thoughts 69
thousands hands 12
time 67
Try your best 20

U

Ullambana 38, 39

V

vow of silence 63
vows 45, 72

W

warning 79
Western Land of Ultimate Bliss 37
womb 62

homepage: http:\\www.drba.org
web-site: www.bttsonline.org